a stroll in the VATICAN GARDENS

TEXTS
BY
E.M. JUNG - INGLESSIS

EDIZIONI Musei Vaticani

Facade of the Casina Pio IV with the statue of the goddes Cybil.

Cover: General view of St. Peter's Dome from the Vatican Gardens, in front of the Fountain of the Sacrament and the Casina Pio IV.

Frontespiece: The emblem of Pope John Paul II in front of the Governatorato.

Back cover: View of the dome of St. Peter's basilica from the rose garden at the top of the Vatican hill.

Translation:
Henry McConnachie

© Copyright 1995.
Ufficio Vendita Pubblicazioni e Riproduzioni Musei Vaticani - Città del Vaticano.

The author wishes to thank the Photographic Archives of the Vatican Museums for their indispensable cooperation in the production of the present volume, as well as the Department of the Vatican Gardens.

Photographs:
Musei Vaticani (Archivio Fotografico - Pietro Zigrossi).

TIPOGRAFIA VATICANA
1995

Introduction

In the urban desert, imprisoned by rivers of asphalt and cement, deafened by the roar of traffic and the thousand and one noises that break the threshold of the decibel limit, the Vatican gardens appear as an oasis of peace and tranquility that in a verdant embrace affectionately enclose Michelangelo's dome. To enjoy this oasis to the full a guide is necessary.

Dr. M. Jung-Inglessis, with her present little book *A Stroll in the Vatican Gardens*, offers us the ideal guide to savour the peace and serenity of this oasis by strolling along its green and fragrant paths in serenity. She enables us to admire the statues and the fountains that add a fresh and wholesome note of art to the fragrance and the colours, but above all she teaches us to prise out the history, both important and not, in which this patch of land is steeped, accompanying it with appropriate anecdotes.

I consider this text by Dr. Jung-Inglessis a very useful aid, but especially a very precious souvenir, for all those who visit the Vatican gardens. In its modest proportions it is an excellent guide, very inspired and suitable for the public who wish to visit the gardens. The authoress does not lose herself in the presentation of bald figures, nor does she bore us with erudite but heavy architectural or historical dissertations. The work is almost like one of those quiet conversations one enjoys on cold winter evenings in front of a glowing hearth. It is like taking the hand of the visitor in an affectionate manner and introducing him gradually, without any rush, into the centuries-old history of the gardens, revealing their secrets and enabling us to enjoy their beauty in a distinctive way.

When I read the manuscript in order to prepare a few words of presentation I was struck by the exact knowledge of the gardens and the love with which they are described. It is a family guide, charming, stimulating and full of optimism and warmth.

These attributes of the book moreover reflect the personality of the authoress who lived for many years in the Vatican which she rightly considers her home, and of which she has pleasant and grateful memories, strengthened by her Christian faith.

I hope that this guide will not only help visitors to enjoy their visit to the gardens, but will also increase their love for the Holy Father and for the Universal Church, of which he is Pastor.

Rosalio J. Cardinal Castillo Lara
President of the Pontifical Commission
for the Vatican City State

The Information Office in St. Peter's Square
where visits to the Vatican Gardens can be booked.

A stroll in the Vatican gardens is at one and the same time a tour of Vatican City State and enables us to have a glimpse inside the smallest country in the world, unique of its kind. It is moreover a journey through 2000 years of history with great historical monuments and works of art. The Vatican is therefore like a marvelous symbiosis of nature and history, of art and religion.

The tour starts on the left, to the south of St. Peter's Square, where a long passageway, the so-called *Charlemagne Wing*, leads to the bell-tower. Here is the *Information Office* where guided tours can be booked. It is not permitted to wander freely inside the Vatican but it is possible, for an entrance fee, to join one of the guided tours which are organized in various languages. This type of visit has only been possible in recent years, at fixed times, when the Pope himself is not using the gardens. Usually the gardens can be visited on Monday, Tuesday, Thursday, Friday and Saturday mornings, either on foot or by bus. Taking the bus one saves time and energy, in that the ascent of the Vatican Hill, which at first cannot be seen, hidden as it is by the imposing mass of St. Peter's Basilica, is much steeper than one would think. The Vatican is only one kilometre long and therefore one could go from one end to the other in about fifteen minutes. But on a tour like this that we plan to take together the things to be seen and described are so many and such that no less than two hours are required.

There are five entrances to the Vatican City State. We shall take the one under the bell-tower, called the *Arch of the Bells*. Two Swiss Guards, their halberds held firmly in their grasp, are on sentry duty. They are wearing the traditional uniform of the lans-

The Arch of the Bells,
one of the four entrances to the Vatican City
supervised by the Swiss Guards.

quenets (a class of mercenary soldiers), with their multicoloured baggy breeches, helmets or berets, as were used when the *Swiss Guard* was founded in 1506. At that time the Swiss were the best mercenaries in Europe and every prince wanted to have his own Swiss bodyguard. So too did Pope Julius II. And the tradition has always been respected since then. There are about a hundred guards and they must be true Swiss citizens. During the course of a solemn ceremony they swear fidelity to the flag and make a pledge to serve the Pontiff for two years, during which they must stay in the barracks, lead an upright life and remain single. The period of service for officers and non-commissioned officers is instead longer and therefore they can get married but they must live in the barracks with their families.

At the other end of the passage we find the gendarmes of the *Corpo di Vigilanza* (Security Corps), as they are officially called. They too number about a hundred, but differently from the Swiss guards they are Italian citizens, they must be tall and they wear a modern dark blue uniform with gilt buttons. Unlike the Swiss guards they are taken on for life and most of them are married, but they live with their families outwith the Vatican as there is not sufficient accommodation inside. The gendarmes are responsible for internal order because even in the most peaceful state in the world one cannot do without policemen. They do not allow anyone to enter the Vatican unless they have the appropriate *tessera* (pass) issued to Vatican residents and employees. Those who want to pay a visit to somebody in the Vatican are first directed to a Permit Office where they have to prove their identity and fill in a form. This rule, however, does not apply to those who are part of a

Square of the Roman Protomartyrs seen from the roof of St. Peter's Basilica. The square is on the site of the ancient Circus of Nero. In the centre to the right of the photograph can be seen the Teutonic College and the Cemetery and to the extreme right the Sacristy and the Chapter House.

group organized by the Information Office. After having passed the controls of the Swiss Guard and the gendarmes without any difficulty, we come to the *Piazza of the Roman Protomartyrs*, called after the first Christian martyrs of Rome. A commemorative plaque records that Nero's Circus stood here and that it was on this spot that the first Christians were martyred. This was after the great fire which in July of the year 64 destroyed the whole centre of the city and for which the Emperor Nero blamed the Christians to avert the suspicions and the anger of the people falling on himself. As was usual, an Egyptian obelisk was raised in the centre of the arena and this remained standing right up to mediaeval times, even after the Circus had long crumbled and fallen into ruin, until the year 1586, when it was moved to the new St. Peter's Square. It still stands there today, as "eyewitness" of what was the first great persecution of the Christians. The original site of the obelisk is marked by a stone slab in the square where we are. And so we can have some idea of the position and size of the Circus. It stretched the whole length of the present St. Peter's Square up to the foot of the Vatican Hill.

On part of this site, that is on the southern side of the former Circus, we now find the *Campo Santo Teutonico*, or Teutonic Ce-

St. Peter's dome seen from the Teutonic Cemetery.

The majolica picture in the Teutonic Cemetery representing the Apostle Peter awaiting martyrdom in Nero's Circus. According to legend, at that moment he had a vision of St. Peter's dome and it was here that it was erected 1500 years later.

metery, and the Collegio Teutonico in Campo Santo. On the outer wall of the building there is a large majolica mosaic depicting the founder, the Emperor Charlemagne. Under the portrait is the proud inscription: *Carolus Magnus me fundavit* (Charlemagne founded me). When the emperor came to Rome, the Pope made him a gift of this land so that he could build a residence, set up a *Schola Francorum,* a hospice for pilgrims from Franconia who were already beginning to pour into Rome. Some of them arrived so worn out and exhausted after the dangers and trials of their long journey over the Alps that they died in Rome and at least wanted to be buried close to the goal of their pilgrimage, that is close to St. Peters tomb. And so the German Cemetery was founded almost spontaneously and even today any pilgrim or Roman resident from a German-speaking country which formerly belonged to the Holy Roman Empire of the Germanic Nation, provided he is a Catholic, can be buried here if he should die in Rome. *Teutones in pace*, Germans in peace, is the consoling and auspicious motto written on the gates of the Cemetery.

It is worth the trouble to take a look inside the Cemetery where its evocative setting in the shadow of St. Peter's dome can almost reconcile us with death. Here we can find the names of famous artists, of distinguished prelates, but also those of humble pilgrims. Worthy of particular interest is a majolica picture placed on the boundary wall. It is not a great work of art, but depicts a beautiful legend: one can see the Apostle Peter surrounded by a group of faithful in Nero's Circus, praying with his hands raised, while awaiting his martyrdom. Suddenly he has a vision: the dome of St. Peter's appears to him above the clouds. It may be that the legend came afterwards, but the fact remains that next to the spot, where St. Peter suffered martyrdom, 1,500 years later the dome was raised over his tomb. We are therefore standing on the most sacred Christian site in Rome, impregnated as it is with the blood of the first martyrs. Legend also has it that the Empress Helena had earth from Mount Golgotha spread over this ground to unite symbolically the blood of Christ with that of the Roman martyrs. Therefore it is a rare privilege that the Teutonic Cemetery is in a place so sacred to Christian history.

Let us stop for a moment at the door of the church. Although the church was built in the year 1500, the bronze door is very recent. In fact one can read: "In praise and honour of Theodor Heuss". Heuss was the first President of the Federal Republic of Germany to visit the Vatican after the Second World War, in 1957, and on that occasion he donated the new door to the church. This is a work by a Cologne artist, Elmar Hillebrand, and includes all the signs of this historic site: below, the resurrection of the dead and above, the rounds of the beati. In the centre appears the Pietà, to whom the church is dedicated and the two-headed Hapsburg eagle, as the church was built under the Hapsburgs, and all the people who originally came from the nations of the former Hapsburg empire still have spiritual citizenship here. On the door knob we can recognize the monogram of Charlemagne, to whom this German institution goes back and which still today constitutes an extraterritorial enclave within the Vatican.

The wings of the *Teutonic College* enclose the small cemetery in a protective embrace.

100 years ago the old hospice for pilgrims became a college for German priests who work and study in the Vatican. It has an important library specialising in Church history and Christian archaeology, as well as a small palaeo-Christian museum. The house is run by the sisters of "Christian Charity" from Paderborn, and a German archconfraternity looks after the Cemetery. Behind the *Cemetery* there rises the white, undulating structure of the new auditorium, a masterpiece of the famous Italian architect, Pierluigi Nervi, inaugurated in 1971 by Pope Paul VI and now called the *Paul VI Hall*. As the confines of the Vatican cannot extend outside the limits established, unfortunately the Hall is unhappily wedged between the Teutonic Cemetery and the Holy Office and cannot be seen as well as it should be. It is in fact a very beautiful construction in the form of a shell with seating for 6,300 and an equal number of standing places. Despite this, these are not sufficient for the large Wednesday general audiences which, weather permitting, are held in St. Peter's Square, or divided into language groups, in the Basilica and in the Hall. The auditorium is also used for other purposes, such as congresses and concerts.

To advance further inside the Vatican we must pass under two small bridges connecting St. Peter's Basilica with the Sacristy. The latter was not included in Michelangelo's design. It was, however, constructed 200 years later by Carlo Marchioni, about the year 1780, and was purposely not incorporated into the Basilica so as not to block the view of Michelangelo's grandiose architecture. It was therefore only connected with the master building by two bridges. With its 43 metre high cupola, the Sacristy alone is as big as a church. Built together with the Sacristy is the Canonica (Chapter House), a tall rectangular building housing the clergy of the Basilica, it too a work by Marchioni.

Behind us we see the *Hospice of St. Martha*, a house built for pilgrims on the occasion of the 1900 Holy Year, and now transformed

Piazza Santa Marta. To the left the Palazzo San Carlo, more to the centre the petrol pump, to the right, hidden among the trees, the Palazzo del Tribunale.

into a residence for priests visiting Rome or working for the Holy See. It is run by French Vincentian sisters.

The next square we come to, like the hospice, is called Piazza Santa Marta, to commemorate an ancient church of this name which was demolished to make way for the new square. It is a wide square with a fountain in the centre surrounded by trees and hedges. The imposing walls of the south transept of the Basilica rise up on the right. This transept is an original work of Michelangelo and he attended to its every particular, so obliging later architects to continue to build in the same style. He was already 70 years old when he was given the commission to construct St. Peter's, so he knew full well that he would never bring his greatest and most important work to completion. Moreover he refused to accept any retribution for it. He said he wanted to build St. Peter's "for the glory of God and for the salvation of my soul".

Let us stop in front of a special side entrance to the Basilica. It is a modern (1972) door of gilded bronze, the work of Lelio Scorzelli. It is called the *Door of Prayer,* as it depicts in relief four of the Church's prayers: the Credo, the Pater Noster, the Ave Maria and the Benedictus. This demonstrates that work always continues in the Basilica and that modern art has found a place in the Vatican as well.

In marked contrast with the high wall of

white travertine of St. Peter's, we see behind it a small church of brownish tones, *St. Stephen of the Abyssinians*. It is the most ancient church in the Vatican and dates back, according to the inscription above the door, to Pope Leo I, that is say, to the fifth century. The portal is framed by a very beautiful Romanesque marble frieze. Originally St. Stephen's was a basilica with three naves; today only the central nave remains with at the sides some ancient columns incorporated into the lateral walls. The gravestones on the walls recall Abyssinian monks and pilgrims who arrived often under great hardship from their distant country, the only one that remained Christian in Africa, and who died here in Rome. Originally the Abyssinian pilgrims lodged in a house alongside the church; in fact in mediaeval times, not only the aforementioned Franks, but almost all the other nations possessed their own *Schola*, or hospice, near St. Peter's. The Abyssinian one was demolished only at the beginning of this century. The church, however, still belongs to them and is still used for religious services in the Coptic-Alexandrine rite.

Piazza Santa Marta is closed to the west by an ochre-coloured building, the *Palazzo del Tribunale*. This houses the judiciary offices and courts, as this minute State has its own laws and judges too, and even its own prison, the only one certainly never overcrowded! The building also houses the father confessors of St. Peter's. They are always Franciscan conventual friars who wear a black habit and are therefore called the "black Franciscans". There is a confessor for each of the main languages, English, German, Spanish, French, Polish etc. Sometimes, especially on Good Friday, the Holy Father takes his place in the confessional.

On the left side of the piazza we find the *Palazzo San Carlo*, built in the last century as a hospital of the sisters of St. Charles Borromeo. Today it is used for offices and apartments. In the courtyard behind there is the St. Pius X Pre-seminary, a so-called minor seminary. Living here are about 30 boys between the ages of 10 and 15. They are boarders, have their own secondary school and earn their keep by serving Mass in St. Peter's from the early hours of the morning. During the summer holidays when they return to their families they are replaced by an equal number of boys from Malta, and so the Maltese have been given the privilege of sending altar-boys to the Vatican during the summer. The boys are extremely proud of carrying out such an important task. At times, during pauses between lessons, they can be heard shouting and playing on the terrace and one wonders how there can be so many children in a supposedly ecclesiastical State. In the gardens above they have a basket-ball court and a tennis court. Outside the walls there is even a football field for Vatican residents and dependents. All that is missing is a swimming pool (there is only one at Castel Gandolfo), but the many large and small fountains give a pleasing sensation of freshness to anyone walking in the gardens.

In front of the *Palazzo San Carlo* there is a petrol station. Where often long queues of cars are filling up. The Vatican, as a sovereign State, can import anything it wants without having to pay customs duty or taxing merchandise. Obviously only those who have the aforementioned tessera can use this pump.

On the opposite side there is the *Piazzetta di Pierluigi da Palestrina*, called after the famous composer and choir-master of St. Peter's, who lived here from 1571 until his death in 1594. On the left there is a narrow side road, the *Vicolo del Perugino*, that also recalls another artist, Perugino, who lived here and who, in the period 1481-1483, painted some of the frescoes in the Sistine Chapel.

Going a little further up the hill we find ourselves in front of the *Studio del Mosaico*, the Vatican's mosaic laboratory. It is a low modest building that looks like a garage; this despite the fact that the Studio can boast of a glorious past. It was founded almost 400 years ago to decorate St. Peter's

S. Stephen of the Abyssinians, the most ancient church in the Vatican with its portal surmounted by a fine marble frieze. In the backgroung can be seen the statue of the Blessed Virgin on the roof of the Governatorato.

Basilica with mosaics, which, as is well known, wear better than paintings. Here restorations of ancient mosaics are carried out and new works produced, like, for example, the portraits of the pontiffs destined for the Basilica of St. Paul Outside the Walls. The school of mosaics can boast of having invented a special procedure: long, fine strips of enamel of different thicknesses are baked and glazed in an oven in 28,000 different shades of colour, then broken up into small pieces and composed into pictures. Here anyone can buy mosaics or order them for their own churches. It is only a question of money as the more subtle the tesserae are, the more laborious the work is and therefore the more costly the mosaic becomes.

There are also three other artistic laboratories at the other side of the Vatican: one for the restoration of the statues and paintings, one for the conservation of manuscripts and ancient books, and the third for the restoration of tapestries. With their patronage the Popes have always encouraged not only great artists but also small artisans, both to ensure their own fame and to promote art, artists and artisans. Moreover, love of art and the desire to build was also a good opportunity to provide new jobs. Besides art, right from mediaeval times, the Popes loved and cared for nature, plants, grasses and flowers, as we shall see when we come to the gardens.

Going up a few paces beyond the Mosaic Studio we reach the Railway Station. A large iron door guarded by two Egyptian sphinges separates the Vatican and Italian railway lines. Once a day the door is opened to allow the goods train, pulled by a small whistling locomotive, to enter. The waggons

come from all over the world. The Vatican provides itself with provisions of foodstuffs, petrol, tobacco, building materials, in short everything that is needed for the day to day life of a small State. In fact when the Vatican City State was created in 1929, Pope Pius XI, to demonstrate the newly acquired independence, had a sumptuous *Railway Station* in travertine and marble built by his court architect, Giuseppe Momo. But it was used only once by a pope for a journey outside Rome, and that is when John XXIII, in 1962, wished to go to Assisi and Loreto by train. As there were no passenger carriage available, however, he had to borrow one from the President of the Italian Republic. For short journeys the Pope travels by car or by helicopter and for longer ones uses an aeroplane. A Philatelic and Numismatic Museum has been installed in the large atrium of the Station.

On the right corner of the building we can see a large number of holes in the wall. They come from the only bombing suffered by the Vatican during the Second World War, when Rome was an "open city" and should not have been subjected to fighting or bombardment. However, on the evening of the 5th November 1943 four bombs fell

 The Railway Station, built by Giuseppe Momo immediately after the foundation of Vatican City State in 1929. The big iron gate on the left separates the Vatican railway from that of the Italian State. The building also houses a numismatic and philatelic museum.

The right corner of the Railway Station; one can see traces of the bombing of the 5th November 1943 during the German occupation.

exactly behind the apse of St. Peter's. All the windows were smashed but the dome, almost by miracle, was undamaged. A few splinters hit the station and the holes remain there to recall that mysterious bombardment. It has never been known who dropped the bombs. Perhaps they were dropped as a warning to the Pope who at that time was giving asylum in the Vatican to many people, of all political parties, races and creeds. How many of these there were, no one will ever be able to say, as great care was taken not to register their names for fear the lists could fall into the hands of the SS.

Looking round now to the right, we see a long building on the side of the hill exactly behind the Basilica. Above on the roof, the statue of the Blessed Virgin who seems to want to hold a conversation with St. Peter who is in front of her. On the lawn at her feet is always depicted the coatof-arms of the reigning pontiff made of flowers and boxwood. John Paul II's is very simple: a yellow cross on a light blue background, and below on the right the letter "M" for Mary. The building is the *Governatorato*, the administrative headquarters, also built by Momo in 1929, for the new State. To have a better understanding of the reason for the Vati-

The Governatorato, the administrative headquarters of the Vatican City State from the time of its foundation in 1929, a work of the architect Giuseppe Momo. Below can be seen the coat of arms of the reigning Pontiff composed of flowers and boxwood.
Above is the Ethiopian College.

can's existence it is necessary to go back to a short chapter in the history of the papacy. For about a thousand years the Pope was not only head of the Church but also sovereign of the Pontifical States, which included a great part of central Italy from the Tyrrhenian Sea to the Adriatic and extended north to include Bologna and south almost to Gaeta. But in 1870 King Victor Emmanuel II took Rome and seized all the Pontifical States. The Pope withdrew inside the Vatican, considering himself a prisoner of the King, and in protest never left for almost 60 years until, with the signing of the Lateran Pacts in 1929, he was reconciled with the King. He solemnly renounced all that in fact had been lost for almost 60 years previously and in compensation the tiny Vatican City was recognized as a sovereign State with the name *Vatican City State*, the initials of which, "SCV" (Stato della Città del Vaticano), appear on the number plates of official Vatican cars. The area of this small State is no more than that of an average sized farm, less than 44 hectares, but the Pope did not intend to possess any more than was absolutely necessary to symbolize and guarantee the sovereignty of the Pontiff. "That bit of territory", Pius XI declared, "without which this sovereignty could not exist, as it would have no place to stand... Only that bit needed to keep body and soul together". And this is precisely the function of the Vatican: to be the bond between the soul and the body, between the Pontiff and the Universal Church. We must however distinguish between the Vatican and the Curia. The Vatican is a geographical entity, it is a locality, and it is a State, whereas the Curia is the collective designation of the ecclesiastical offices (dicasteries) of the universal Church. The dicasteries have an international character and are not identified with the Vatican City State although for the most part they have their headquarters there.

The Vatican State is a *unicum* in every sense. It is the only elective monarchy still in existence. In fact the Pope is elected by the cardinals in conclave and then becomes the absolute sovereign for life of this small State. To ensure that it would be well run, Pius XI nominated a Governor for whom the *Governatorato* was built. When the governor died the vacancy was not filled, and the Vatican is now administered by a Pontifical Commission that acts in the Pope's name, presided over by a Cardinal, and assisted by a *Special Delegate* and a *Consulta*. It administers about 500 residents (about 100 of whom are women, including wives, house-keepers and sisters, and about 50 children) and some 2,000 dependents who work but not reside in the Vatican as there is no accommodation for them inside. The residents in their turn are sub-divided into two categories: citizens with Vatican passports and citizenship (cardinals court functionaries, officials, diplomats) and residents without citizenship. They are of different nationalities, professions and languages: what unites them is not their identity of origin, language or culture, but the service they render to the Pontiff and therefore to the universal Church. When they are no longer in service they must leave the Vatican. As long as they are living here they enjoy many advantages; they live in official apartments and do not pay any taxes as the Pope does not require them. The men are not conscripted for military service as the Vatican does not have an army. Housewives and pensioners do their shopping at a reduced price in the Annona, that is the internal supermarket, and the children can play undisturbed in the Pope's garden.

Behind the *Governatorato* there is a "Steingarten", a rock garden with an artificial grotto called the Fountain of the Reef. Above, in an idyllic green setting, there is the *Ethiopian College*, the only college inside the Vatican apart from the Teutonic College which we have already spoken

The Fountain of the Reef in the rock garden along the avenue that runs behind the Governatorato.

The Fountain of the Shell in the Italian garden.

about. It also was built in the same year, 1929, and by the same architect, Momo, who designed the *Governatorato* and the Railway Station. When Pius XI was asked why exactly the Ethiopians should have a seminary in the Vatican, he replied with a smile: "Because a little black looks good on white", referring to the dark skin of the Abyssinians. In our day, however, they have had difficulty in leaving their country and this is why the sisters of the Congregation of the Child Mary, who now work in the Vatican offices, have "requisitioned" a wing of this beautiful building constructed in the form of a horseshoe. It was only after the Second Vatican Council that women, preferably sisters, were assumed in the Vatican. They are employed in the various dicasteries, they are announcers on Vatican Radio and run the central telephone exchange.

The road that goes from the Station to the Ethiopian College is rather steep but shaded by evergreen ilexes. On the left, on the slope of the hill behind the Station, we can immediately see a large shell-shaped fountain surrounded by a green arabesque border. A little further up we find a labyrinth of high hedges of boxwood. These hedges are characteristic of the so-called "Italian" garden style, which as its name implies started in Italy and more precisely in the 16th century when, with the beautiful Renaissance villas, garden architecture was also born, in accordance with the ideal of harmony between palace and landscape. The plants were no longer allowed to grow as nature intended but pruned to follow precise geometric forms. This type of garden consists solely of green plants: trees, bushes, hedges, and the art lies in harmonizing their different tones and shades of green. Tall pines and cypresses, cedars and chestnuts alternate with magnolias, jew and mimosa. The paths are framed by evergreen ilexes and almost every species of palm grows there: from the tall date-palm to the pointed Cycas, to the low *Chamaerops humilis*, which are called here St. Peter's palms. These are trees typical of a Mediterranean environment but we also find clumps of African bananas, Japanese ginkgo trees, and Australian monkey-puzzles which throw their amusing bushy crowns up to the sky.

This arrangement of the southern slope of the hill was made only this century when the new Vatican City State was founded and was conceived as a garden-city, in which almost half of the total territory should consist of green areas.

Having arrived at the top of the hill, we find ourselves in the "French" garden which is different from the Italian one as it is decorated with flowers. Here we can see multi-coloured flower-beds and flower borders surrounding the green lawns and large urns filled with flowers scattered almost everywhere. Each season produces different flowers: spring, the red-pink camellias, summer, the purple bougainvillaea and autumn, the pale blue plumbago. Everywhere there are large oleander bushes of different colours: white, pink and dark red. Every now and again a solitary agave thrusts up a very tall single stem crowned with little yellow flowers before withering all together. But the most beautiful spot is the rose-garden along the crest of the hill. Through archways of highly-perfumed jasmine and pink roses one can enjoy a magnificent panorama of the whole city and when visibility is good one can see as far as the Alban Hills where at Castel Gandolfo, 25 km. to the south, the Pope has his summer residence. It is only from here that we can admire in all its grandeur the cupola of St. Peter's, the cupolone (the big dome), as the Romans proudly call it; in fact from the front it is masked by the tall mass of the church portico. It is necessary to stand here to understand how the church should have appeared in accordance with Michelangelo's design: a central building with four equal arms and in the centre a cupola which should be visible in the same way from every side. Seen from where we are the cupola seems to symbolize God's blessing and protective hands, reaching out exactly above the tomb of St. Peter to preserve it up to the present day. The cupola has the form of a tiara, almost as if it were the tiara of the first Pope, who in fact was St. Peter. His tomb is exactly the heart and focal point of the Vatican which in its 2000 years of history developed around it in so many concentric circles. Wherever we go we are always walking around the cupola and wherever we turn our gaze it is always the cupola that dominates our vision; at times it appears between the trees or above the rooftops or, again, it suddenly comes into sight at the end of an avenue. St. Peter's tomb which lies below is not only the heart and the symbol of the Vatican, it is also the basis of its existence, its raison d'être, as the Popes live here for only one reason: because here is the tomb of their first predecessor and tradition demands that all his successors should reside here and possibly also be buried in the same place.

The so-called *Labyrinth*, characteristic of an Italian garden. Behind the Ethiopian College in the background St. Peter's Dome.

Behind us loom the high Leonine Walls, so-called because they were built by Leo IV (847-855), to protect St. Peter's Basilica from the incursions of the Saracens; starting from the Tiber the walls rise up as far as the hill and surround it. We must not in fact forget that the Vatican hill was not one of the classic seven hills of Rome but was outside the ancient city walls beyond the Tiber. The Etruscans originally lived on this bank of the river. The word *vaticanum* probably comes from the Etruscan and has something to do with *vatica, vaticum and vaticinium*, that is with "prophecy". When the Romans advanced beyond the Tiber and destroyed the land of the Etruscans this became a deserted, unhealthy and infamous spot. Tacitus speaks about the *infamibus vaticani locis*,

The Leonine Walls, at the top of the Vatican hill, erected around the year 850 under Leo IV for the protection of St. Peter's Basilica. The walls lead to the Vatican Radio Tower. At the centre of the little square the statue of St. Austremonius, the first bishop of Alvernia, a gift from his diocese of Clermont in France.

about the infamous Vatican places (*Historiae* II, 93, 2); Pliny the Elder, in his *Historia Naturalis*, VIII, 37, recounts that in the undergrowth here there lived gigantic serpents that could swallow a child in one gulp. The wine produced in this area was so acid that Martial in his Epigrams (VI, 92 and X, 45) said ironically "*vaticana bibis; bibis venenum... vaticana bibas si delectaris aceto*" (if you drink Vatican wine you drink poison... if you like vinegar you can drink the wine of the Vatican). Things improved when Agrippina, the mother of the Emperor Caligula, planted beautiful gardens here and her son built a circus or stadium for chariot races. This was inherited by Nero and was therefore also called Nero's Circus, in which the first martyrs were put to death, as we said at the beginning. Alongside the Circus there developed a cemetery for pagans and Christians, rich and poor alike. This necropolis was then levelled on the orders of the Emperor Constantine when about the year 320 he had the first basilica built on the site of the tomb of Peter. It was, however, outside the walls of the city, without any protection whatsoever and therefore at the mercy of all plunderers. It was only after Leo IV had those high walls built that people were able to find a safe dwelling: pilgrims, merchants, artisans and clerics came to settle there. During the Middle Ages a real city developed within the walls and it was called the Leonine City and later the Vatican City. Behind, to the west, there was only the "Valley of Hell" an uncultivated piece of land which stretched as far as the sea. To the east, the Tiber separated it from the city of Rome. The Vatican is still referred to today as being "beyond the Tiber", although in the meantime Rome developed around it, so much so that in our time the Vatican

The Lourdes Grotto, a faithful reproduction of the Grotto of Massabielle near Lourdes presented by the French in 1902 to Leo XIII whose portrait in mosaic can be seen up on the left; on the right the portrait of Bishop Schoepfer of Tarbes-Lourdes. The altar is the original one from Lourdes sent to John XXIII in 1958 on the occasion of the centenary of the apparitions of Our Lady of Lourdes.

City is within another city, it is a State within another State—a development that could not have been foreseen and now strips us of the illusion of having arrived here at the end of the inhabited world.

After a few metres the walls are interrupted by a square in which in 1902 the French built the *Lourdes Grotto,* a very faithful reproduction of the grotto at Massabielle. The original idea for the undertaking came from the bishop of Tarbes, Mons. Schoepfer, in whose diocese Lourdes is situated. That is why he is portrayed in a mosaic medallion at the top on the right, while on the opposite side there is another of Leo XIII, to whom the grotto was donated. The altar in the centre was in the grotto of Massabielle for a hundred years before being moved here in 1958. The Popes occasionally celebrate mass here, for example, for the Vatican gardeners or for the sick who are brought here in wheel-chairs. In May and October there are Marian devotions and candlelight processions which wend their way from the bottom of the hill right up to the grotto. Pilgrims and visitors often stop here to pray and to sing hymns. In former times the grotto was surmounted by a neo-gothic tower which has now disappeared.

The Leonine Walls were restored by Nicholas V (1447-1455), who added the battlements and towers. The one on the left, to the south, is called "*St. John's Tower*". The name refers to both John the Baptist and John the Evangelist, both of whom are depicted above the entrance. The name can also refer to Pope John XXIII who made this tower his hermitage; and so his coat-of-arms also appears above the entrance. Unfortunately he was able to enjoy the ro-

The Leonine Walls and the Tower of St. John seen from the French garden.

the avenues asphalted. Pius XII, on the contrary, walked the length of this little wall every day at a fixed time, even when it was rainy and windy, and was sheltered by a glass covering on each side. He always walked alone and did not want to be disturbed by anyone because he took advantage of that hour to study his documents and to prepare his discourses. John XXIII, instead, did not like to go for walks on his own and did not want to be tied down to fixed times. He liked to sit in the company of his

The Tower of St. John formed part of the mediaeval walls. It was arranged by John XXIII as his hermitage; now it serves as a residence for guests of honour of the Pope. Above the entrance can be seen the coat of arms of John XXIII, to the right the figure of John the Baptist and on the left that of John the Evangelist.

mantic peace of the tower only for a few days: he fell seriously ill and died shortly afterwards on the 3rd June 1963. Today St. John's Tower is used to house important guests of the Pope, like for example, the Patriarch of Constantinople, as there are no hotels in the Vatican.

A low wall covered with climbing plants starts at the tower and meets the Leonine Walls at a right angle. This wall has a story of its own. It is known that every Pope has his own habits. Leo XIII liked to sit in front of his own little house on the hill. Benedict XV preferred to stop in front of the shrine of Our Lady of the Guard from his native city of Genoa. Pius XI moved around the gardens only by car and therefore had

The Chinese Pavilion, a gift of the Chinese Catholics in 1933.
It was John XXIII's favourite resting place
when the pavilion still had walls, windows and furniture.

secretary in a Chinese pavilion at the other end of the park, in the socalled English garden. Unfortunately only the roof now remains. His successor, Paul VI, did not like to walk in the gardens. Instead he had a hanging-garden laid out above his apartment where he could go quickly any time he wished using the lift. As Vatican gardens were not used by the Pope, it was decided to open them to the public, fixing, however, an entrance fee to help the costs of maintenance. However, when John Paul II, a sportsman, ascended the pontifical throne he wanted to use the gardens for exercise.

And so they were once more closed to the public. Today, one must always enquire beforehand if it is possible to visit at a specific time or if the gardens are being used by the Pope or by some special visitor.

When the Leonine Walls began to deteriorate new ones were built parallel to them, but these are already 400 years old. They were to provide protection for St. Peter's Basilica and the pontifical palace, but since 1929 they also mark the confines of the new Vatican City State. They have a trapezoid shape and a perimeter of 3,420 metres. For some years now, at the spot where the walls

The Pope disembarks from a helicopter in the Vatican's little heliport.

form an acute angle, near St. John's Tower, there is the Vatican airport. To tell the truth it is only a heliport, only big enough to allow a helicopter to take off and land. Now, when he goes to Castel Gandolfo and when he returns to Rome for the audiences the Pope uses this means of transport which is quicker and safer, also avoiding blocking the already chaotic city traffic still further. Now official visitors also arrive often by helicopter.

We are now exactly at the highest point of the Vatican hills, 78 metres above sea level, and at the extreme limit of the State. From the border-line below in St. Peter's Square to here, the Vatican measures exactly one kilometre 45 metres and at its broadest point 850 metres. It is therefore only a State in miniature, and yet it is a model State in that it has all it needs: its own passports, a postal service, newspapers, shops, a supermarket workshops and petrol pumps, a credit institute, a radio station, even a railway station and for some time now the aforementioned heliport.

Hugging the outer walls along an olive-lined avenue, we can hear the roar of the great city which rises up like waves breaking against high reefs without, however, being able to breach them.

On our right, between the Leonine Walls and the boundary wall, stands a rather big monument in white marble sculptured by A. Ponzanelli and donated by the Mexicans to Pius XII in 1939. It represents the apparition of *Our Lady of Guadalupe* in 1531 on the mantle of the poor Indian, Juan Diego, while the bishop of Mexico City, the Franciscan, Juan de Zumarraga, kneels down before her.

A few steps further on we find another monument on our left, this time in bronze, by Frederick Shrado from New York. It represents *Our Lady of Fatima* who inclines for-

The apparition of *Our Lady of Guadalupe*. The marble group by A. Ponzanelli was a gift from the Mexican Catholics in 1939. The tower of St. John is on the left.

ward in a gesture of protection over a small group of people. Engraved on the plinth is the date the 13th May 1981, the feast of Our Lady of Fatima and very the day of the attempt on the life of Pope John Paul II, whose life was spared thanks to the protection of Our Lady. Therefore this monument is intended to be a reminder and at the same time an act of thanksgiving.

Between the two monuments there is a graceful fountain, named the Fountain of the Frogs. Four green frogs are crouching on the edge of the basin and jets of water gush from their mouths.

Having reached the northern extremity of the Leonine Walls we find a second tower, the *Leonine Tower*, which was the headquarters of the Vatican Observatory from 1906 until 1932 when it was transferred to Castel Gandolfo. Today the tower is used for transmissions by Vatican Radio and is therefore called the *Radio Tower*. Vatican Radio was set up in 1931 by the inventor of radio, Guglielmo Marconi, and was originally housed in a low building at the foot of the Leonine Walls, in the so-called *Palazzina Marconi*, which very soon became too small when the Vatican Radio became a large organization with about 400 employees and 34 language sections. The Leonine Tower now houses the administration, while the studios are in a building facing the Castel Sant'Angelo and the large transmission centre was

Our Lady of Fatima, a gift from the artist Frederick Shradi of New York in remembrance of the attack on John Paul II on the 13th May 1981, the anniversary of the apparition of Our Lady of Fatima.

The Fountain of the Frogs, in the French garden.

The Tower of Vatican Radio seen from the rose garden. One can glimpse the bas-relief of Leo XIII with Bismarck.

The bronze bas-relief by the Spanish sculptor F. Ferrer in 1887 to commemorate the treaty on the Caroline Islands stipulated in the Vatican between Germany (represented by Chancellar Bismarck and the Emperor Wilhelm I) and Spain (represented by the Prime Minister Canovas and King Alfonso XII). In the centre Leo XIII and the Secretary of State Cardinal Jacobini.

moved 25 km. outside Rome to the north, to S. Maria di Galeria.

Towards the end of the last century Leo XIII (1878-1903) had a summer villa built alongside the tower. This was the time of the cold war between the Pope and the King, when the Pope could never leave the Vatican but wanted, nevertheless, to have a change of scenery and a breath of fresh air in the summer. His presence here is recorded in a bronze bas-relief on the outside wall of his former residence. To our surprise we notice the "Iron Chancellor", Bismarck, turning towards Pope Leo XIII, while behind him we can see the Kaiser Wilhelm I, with his inevitable helmet and large moustaches. How is it that we find these two Prussian Protestants in the Pope's garden? In reality they were never here. The bas-relief, however, records an historic event, a short chapter in German and Spanish history. After the failure of the so-called "Kulturkampf", Bismarck initiated his colonial policies and had the Prussian navy occupy the unarmed Caroline Islands, a Spanish possession in the Pacific—a precedent for the Falkland Islands. The action unleashed a storm of protests and raised the spectre of war breaking out. Then with great skill Bismarck turned to the Pope and asked him to mediate; and in fact a compromise was reached through the Cardinal Secretary of State Jacobini, who appears on the relief behind the papal throne. This is why we see the Pope, seated at the centre, handing over the same document to both the Spanish Prime Minister, Canovas del Castillo, and to the German Chancellor, Bismarck. This agreement which was dated the 17th December 1885 guaranteed Spain's sovereignty over the islands but Germany obtained the right to berth her ships there, to engage in commerce and to buy land. In the background we can recognize the Emperor Wilhelm I and the King of Spain Alfonso XII shaking hands, thus sealing the accord that had been reached, while the Kaiser gives a friendly pat to the King's shoulder. At the right edge can also be seen three Capuchins who were entrusted with the evangelization of the islands. No one could have suspected that this accord would not last more than 15 years. In fact Spain was then so impoverished that she peacefully sold the Carolines to Germany. After a further fifteen years, however, at the end of the First World War, it was the turn of Germany to be on her knees and she lost these islands once again.

A rare example of the Brazilian national tree the Ceibo (Coral Tree); it was part of Leo XIII's now almost defunct botanical garden.

At present they are under United States mandate. The bas-relief is the work of a Spanish artist who was then working in Rome, as reads in the lower right corner: "The brother of the Servant of God, Sister Filomena of the Minims – Felice Ferrer".

The inscription below explains how and why the work was commissioned. It was donated to Leo XIII in 1887 by the archdioceses of Acerenza and Matera for the golden jubilee of his ordination to the priesthood. On that occasion the Pope received many gifts from all over the Catholic world to compensate him in some way for the loss of his temporal power. And so this bas-relief was intended to pay homage to the Pontiff

⇨
One of the many hedges of dwarf palms (Chamaerops humilis), also called St. Peter's palms or fan palms.

The Mater Ecclesiae Monastery of the Poor Clare Sisters,
recently founded between the botanical garden and the Pope's orchard.

as prince of peace and arbiter between nations and sovereigns. This is why it was placed here, on the outer wall of Leo XIII's former summer residence.

We also owe the present lay out of this part of the gardens to this same Pope. Prior to this, to the north, there was only an orchard and a vegetable garden, called the *pomerium* or *viridarium*, for the daily needs of the court of Nicholas III (1277-1280), the first Pope to take up a fixed abode in the Vatican. First of all a garden of "simples" was added, that is of medicinal plants used by Simone da Genova, the personal physician of Nicholas IV (1288-1292). This was the first botanical garden ever to be established in Italy. A vineyard was then planted and a small leafy wood developed, the *boschetto*. But a true and proper monumental garden was created only at the time of the Renaissance, exactly inside the inner courtyard between the two long corridors that connected the winter palace in St. Peter's Square and the little summer palace, called the *Palazzetto del Belvedere*, on the extreme northern hill. This garden was composed of three sloping terraces; in the third courtyard below there were often equestrian tournaments and theatrical performances; today it has been reduced to a car park for Vatican employees and visitors. When the Pontiffs moved to the Quirinal, the Vatican lost its importance and the gardens were neglected a little. It was only in 1870, when the Popes lost all their external possessions that Leo XIII had new gardens laid out behind the basilica. He also planted a botanical garden, of which only a few exotic trees remain, for example in the little square in front of the Radio a solitary Erythrina (or *Erythryna Cristagalli*), the national tree of South America, in particular of Brazil. It is said that its red petals owe their colour to the blood of an Indian princess who was murdered. Leo XIII also had a small zoo, but today there are at the most a few stray cats, birds, frogs or lizards. At that time the animals could wander about freely. It is said that one day a gazelle leapt out in front of Pope Leo, but he calmly said to his amazed companions: "A lion should not be afraid of a gazelle!", jokingly referring to his own name. He also wanted to produce his own wine, but strangely enough the grapes were always picked by an unknown hand before the harvest. He therefore gave up the idea. Besides, it was known from ancient times that the wine of the Vatican was as acid as vinegar.

Going down now from the Radio Tower along the ancient Leonine Walls covered with bright bougainvillaea, we see a newly built little Church and convent dedicated to the *Mater Ecclesiae* where a few nuns of the Clarissin order from different countries are leading a strict life of pionyer. On the right side, hidden behind a tall laurel hedge, we find a little orchard, the Pope's orchard. Although he has a farm at Castel Gandolfo, this little orchard serves for his daily needs. Through a little gate we can see rows of salads, tomatoes and peas, lemon and orange trees and in the background, in strange contrast, the cupola.

Below the Pope's orchard we come across a bronze statue by Filippo Guaccarini. The two keys indicate that it is of the Apostle Peter. They are keys of the Kingdom of Heaven entrusted by Christ to His vicar. Usually one is gold-coloured and the other silver. This is why the Vatican flag is white and yellow, representing the colours of the two most precious metals and so the keys of St. Peter. The statue was erected to record the First Vatican Council and was placed first of all in the Courtyard of the Pine Cone, atop a tall column that rose above the roofs of the surrounding buildings. It gave such a bizarre impression that when the column began to crack the statue was moved without it to the garden. Here the statue of St. Peter stands high up and isolated with

⇨
The Pope's little orchard
with a view of St. Peter's dome.

Angels that adorned the monument commemorating the First Vatican Council, 1869-1870.

⇦
St. Peter blessing his church. A bronze statue by F. Gnaccarini, the central part of a monument commemorating the First Vatican Council.

his right hand raised in a sign of benediction directed towards his church. At its feet there are four heads of angels in very white marble that belonged to the original monument.

There are many other monuments scattered throughout the gardens which, even if they are not always beautiful, somehow or other reflect the taste of their times. The French donated different statues of saints from their country, often in cast iron as was the fashion at the end of the last century. An exception is the marble statue of St. Theresa of Lisieux placed here in 1927 on the wishes of Pius XI as "custodian of the Vatican

The shrine of St. Theresa of Lisieux, a gift from the Saint's elder sister to Pius XI in 1927 who called St. Theresa the "custodian of the Vatican gardens".

The Little Temple of Our Lady of the Guard, a reproduction of the shrine that guards the port of Genoa. A gift to Pope Benedict XV from his native city in 1917.

The Little Temple of Our Lady of the Guard, detail; the Blessed Virgin appears to the peasant Pareto, a marble group by G. B. Conti, 1917.

St. Peter in Chains, detail of the marble statue by Amalia Dupre from Florence, offered to Leo XIII in 1887, as an allusion to his "imprisonment in the Vatican".

Apollo playing his lyre. This ancient statue, a copy of a Hellenistic original, is in the boschetto.

Gardens". The Genoese in 1917 had, in their turn, sent a copy of the little temple of "Our Lady of the Guard", that dominates the port of Genoa, to their fellow-citizen Benedict XV, so that he would feel less far away from his birthplace. Statues of pagan divinities and busts of Roman emperors seem at their ease amongst angels and saints. Fragments of ancient sarcophagi, marble columns and terra cotta urns are dotted among the greenery. Some of the monuments have given rise to polemics. For example, there is a statue of St. Peter, seated, tired and in chains, with a very sad air, that alludes to the Popes' imprisonment in the Vatican. It is the work of a Florentine sculptress, Amalia Dupré. A marble basrelief represents the First Vatican Council and another exalts the 1864 Syllabus with the allegorical figure of Truth crushing the demon of heresy under its feet. These two bas-

An overall view of the north-west part of the gardens with the Leonine Walls, the Radio Tower, The Fountain of the Eagle, the Statue of St. Peter and the Gardener's House.

The Gardener's House. the residence of the head-gardener, with a little tower which has remained from the first residence fortified by the Popes in the Vatican dating back to the time of Innocent III (1198-1216).

reliefs are the work of Pietro Galli and belonged to the base of the aforementioned Column of the Council but now rest against a little brown house with a small tower that probably dates back to the first Vatican fortifications built under Innocent III (1198-1216). Today it is called the *Gardener's House* as it is the residence of the head gardener who, with the help of 25 under gardeners, looks after the Vatican gardens in an exemplary manner.

The Gardener's House and the statue of St. Peter are in the northern part of the gardens. Here the third style of garden, the English style, predominates. With its complex of leafy trees the so-called "*boschetto*" was intentionally left in its natural state so that when the Pope went for walks there he would have the illusion that he was in the open country. Here one can listen to the gushing of streams, the tinkle of little cascades, the murmuring of countless fountains; the most grandiose is the *Fountain of the Eagle*. It is in the form of an artificial grotto with an eagle perching on top while below two griffins spout water into an oval basin. The eagle and the griffin, that is a winged

The Fountain of the Eagle in the boschetto, built by Jan van Santen (Vasanzio) for Paul V Borghese (1605-1621) with an eagle perched on the top of an artificial grotto and two griffins spurting water into an oval basin. The eagle and griffin are the heraldic animals of the Borghese coat of arms.
To the left is the Claritian Convent and the headquarters of Vatican Radio.

The Casina Pio IV or *Villa Pia*, the upper facade. The Casina was built by Pirro Ligori (1558-62) for Pope Pius IV, a Medici. It now houses the Pontifical Academies of Sciences and Social Studies.

Casina Pio IV: a putto in the fountain in the middle of the inner oval courtyard.

dragon, together form the coat-of-arms of the Borghese family, to which Paul V (1605-1621) belonged. His name is inscribed in large letters on the facade of St. Peter's Basilica, because it was completed during his reign. His court architect was the Dutchman Jan van Santen, whose Italianized name was Vasanzio. He became famous under this name for having built the Casino in the Villa Borghese. Most of the fountains in the Vatican are his work. He restored the ancient aqueduct of the Emperor Trajan which from Lake Bracciano, 39 km. north of Rome, carries water to the Vatican and still today is known by that Pope's name, the "*Acqua Paola*". Thanks to the many fountains and to the automatic sprinklers, the Vatican gardens, even during the most torrid heat of the summer, when everything around is all dried up, are a verdant oasis of freshness.

Under the *boschetto*, we find, graciously nestling on the side of the hill, an enchanting little building started in 1558 under Paul IV and completed in 1561 under

The Casina Pio IV seen from the little square in front with the cupola in the background. The lower facade is decorated with mosaics and stuccoes and three ancient statues: Cybele in the centre, Juventas and Pudicizia on the sides.

Casina Pio IV: the inner oval courtyard, also called the Nymphaeum, unites the four architectural bodies of the Villa.

Casina Pio IV: the frescoed ceiling of the Assembly Hall with the coat of arms of Pope Pius IV, a Medici.

Pius IV. From the latter it took its name the *Villa Pia* or the *Casina di Pio IV*. It was built by Pirro Ligorio who was at the same time a garden architect and hydraulic engineer. His works (the most famous is the Villa d'Este at Tivoli) are always immersed in the landscape and surrounded by the murmuring of water. Art and nature harmoniously combine in the most beautiful jewel-box of

The Fountain of the Sacrament, representing an altar with candles and a monstrance in the centre. The heraldic animals, the eagle and griffin, indicate that it was made under Paul V, a Borghese.

the Renaissance, more precisely described as late Mannerism. The external walls are decorated with stucco bas-reliefs depicting mythological scenes and mosaics in the grotesque style. The ceilings are painted in fresco by Zuccari and Barocci. Three ancient statues, the pagan goddess Cybele and the allegories of *Juventus* and *Pudicitia* are reflected in the water of a fish-pond below. A nymphaeum, an internal oval courtyard, connects the four wings of the building, in which marble putti ride dolphins that spurt water into a similarly shaped oval basin, forming what appears here for the first time in architecture, thus preceding baroque art. It was here that Pius IV used to enjoy moments of peace and his nephew, St. Charles Borromeo, then Cardinal Secretary of State, held his literary evenings. Today the Casina serves a purely scientific purpose: it is the headquarters of the Pontifical Academy of Sciences, instituted in 1936 by Pius XI. Every year the most distinguished scientists from all over the world meet here to examine together actual problems in the field of the natural sciences. Presently it houses the Pontifical Academy of Sciences.

Placing oneself at the left side of the little square in front of the Casina Pio IV one has the most beautiful view of the whole garden: in one single glance we can embrace the very beautiful facade of the Villa with its statues, its mosaics and stuccoes, surrounded by the joyful cascading of water, and in the background the dome of St. Peter's towards which a majestic pine inclines. Once again history, nature and art combine in a unique and marvellous composition.

Facing the Casina di Pio IV a long three storied gallery, a work designed by Bramante, leads from the Apostolic Palace to the Belvedere. The Vatican art collection now extends along the whole passage. Half

The Mint, now serves in part as a store-house for the Floreria Apostolica and partly as residences for Curia prelates. In the background can be seen the Arch of the Sentinel and to the right the great mass of the tower housing the Sistine Chapel.

The Arch of the Sentinel, guarded by a gendarme, is the entry to the apostolic palaces from the garden side.

way along we find the Tower of the Winds, where the original Vatican Observatory was housed. Here the reform of our calendar, the Gregorian calendar, was worked out in detail; it was thus called after Gregory XIII, who introduced it in 1582. At the foot of the tower is the Vatican Secret Archive and behind it the Vatican Library. There are also two schools here: one of Palaeography, Diplomacy and Archive Sciences and the other of Library Sciences, accessible to anyone who has the necessary basic qualifications.

A little further to the right there is another fountain built under Pius V by Vasanzio: the *Fountain of the Sacrament*, that is the sacrament of the altar. It depicts in fact an altar on which four vertical jets of water give the effect of candles, while a griffin projects water in an aureole that appears like a monstrance. The fountain is attached to a yellow-tinted building called the *Pontifical Mint*. The Vatican in fact coins its own money. Every year a new series of coins is issued but as the Vatican Mint was not very profitable it is the Italian State Mint that now strikes the Vatican coins. The building is now used partly for private apartments and partly for the *Floreria Apostolica*, a term that it is not easy to define. It is a large warehouse where everything that can be used to decorate different premises on special occasions is stored: furniture, carpets, wall-hangings, paintings and much more, including the famous stove in which the voting slips used during conclaves are burned.

Beside the Mint there is the *Bakery*, now no longer in use. It has been transformed into offices, but the area in front is still called the *Piazza del Forno* (Bakery Square), and has a beautiful fountain attributed to Maderno. Here we find ourselves at the *Arco della Sentinella* (Arch of the Sentinel), behind and at the foot of the Apostolic Palaces, but a gendarme stops us from passing through. We can only take a look through the Arch and note a vista of courtyards and towers going as far as the Courtyard of St. Damasus, where right at the back there are the Pontiff's private apartments. It is a glance back into the past, to mediaeval times, when the Vatican was still a fortress.

Originally the Popes did not reside in the Vatican but in the Lateran, because the former, being situated outwith the city, was considered to be too insecure. The Popes went to St. Peter's only for special events, like for example, the coronation of an emperor. For this reason they had a secondary lodging built, an *episcopium*, which was gradually developed and fortified. As we have already said the first Pope to take up permanent residence in the Vatican was Nicholas III (1277-1280). Shortly afterwards the Popes moved to Avignon and in the meantime the Lateran Palace fell into ruin. Having returned finally to Rome in 1377, the Popes could no longer live in the Lateran and had to settle between the walls and the towers around the Basilica of St. Peter. Each Pope added what he required from time to time. This is why the Vatican is today an irregular complex of different buildings, built not by one Pope or designed by only one architect, but which sprung up during the centuries and is always being extended and transformed.

We are still close to the Arch of the Sentinel. Looking up, we can see on the right a massive fortified tower with battlements and arrow-slits, built by Sixtus IV (1471-1484). This houses the court chapel, the famous Sistine Chapel, which is also where conclaves are held. At present on the roof there is no sign of the famous chimney which is put in place only on the occasion of a conclave to communicate to the outside world, through the colour of the smoke, what is happening inside: black smoke means the cardinals have not reached agreement; white smoke signifies instead: *habemus Papam*, we have a Pope.

Now we can go round the apse of the basilica and return to the exit or, if we have time, we can make another tour to the northern extremity of the Vatican. To do this we must follow the *Viale del Giardino Quadrato* (the Avenue of the Square Garden) which, passing in front of the wood, leads to the *Picture Gallery*. It is a construction in red brick with majolica decoration, designed in the 1930's by the architect Luca Beltrami. In front of it there is a large square lawn which reminds us of what has remained of

The Square Garden; under the lawn there is the subterranean Historical Museum. On the left the Picture Gallery, in the corner under the pine the Museum cafeteria. Still further on the Palazzetto del Belvedere. In front the long gallery that leads to the apostolic palaces. Half way along the Tower of the Winds with below it the Secret Archive and the Vatican Library.

the "Square Garden". Created by Paul III (1534-1549), it was originally called the "Secret Garden" because it was surrounded by a high wall to protect the Pope from prying eyes while he was taking his walks between the clipped hedges. Below the lawn there is now a large subterranean exhibitions hall, called the Carriage Museum, where one can admire not only the gilded coaches of the Popes when they were sovereigns of Rome, but also the earliest motor-cars: a Graham Page (1929), a Citroën (1929) and a Mercedes Benz (1930), all of them given as gifts to Pope Pius XI.

Running parallel to the Picture Gallery there is a very modern white building, the *Pauline Museum,* inaugurated by Paul VI in 1970 and constructed by the Passarelli Brothers to house the art collections which were previously in the Lateran, in particular, the Museum of early Christian art. Large windows enable us to see below a mosaic pavement from the Baths of Caracalla, representing a series of athletes flexing their muscles, following the taste of the Emperor Caracalla.

The Palazzetto del Belvedere, erected for Innocent VIII (1484-1492), houses the nucleus of the collection of the Vatican Museums' ancient statues.

In the past there was an orange grove here. Now all that remains is an ancient matron in marble with a neck that is too long and a head that is not hers, seated above a fountain. In a way that is not too reverent she is called "the Spinster". Behind this there was once a *gallinarium*, a hen-run, but now there are garden sheds and green-houses, among which there rises up a Renaissance tower which still bears the coat-of-arms of the Cybo Pope, Innocent VIII (1484-1492). To the right here are the new extensive warehouses for the supermarket, called the *Vignaccia*, perhaps to recall the poor vineyards that were here in ancient times.

Only quite recently a multi-coloured fragment of the "Berlin Wall", 3.8 metres high and 1.2 metres wide, was erected here; it was given to the Pope in 1990 in recognition of his moral role in the demolition of the "Iron Curtain" that divided Europe. Significantly this piece of Wall has been placed along the *Viale San Benedetto* (the Avenue of St. Benedict), the co-patron of Europe. Alongside it a marble stone has

The Berlin Wall: this piece was donated to John Paul II in recognition of his spiritual contribution to the collapse of the Berlin Wall. Alongside a stone with the prophetic words of the Pope pronounced in the inaugural address of his pontificate, 1978.

The Fountain of the Spinster: an ancient statue that has given its name to this whole area of the Vatican.

The Fountain of the Galleon dates back to the time of Paul V; the galleon was perhaps made by Jan van Santen (Vasanzio) but restored at various times, the last by Pius XI as can be seen from his coat of arms on the pennant flying from the main mast.

been placed with the prophetic words that John Paul II pronounced in the inaugural discourse of his pontificate on the 9th of November 1978: "Do not be afraid! Open the doors—rather, throw the doors wide open to Christ! Open the borders of the States, their economic systems as well as their political systems. Do not be afraid!". The donor's name is indicated at the base: Marco Piccinini.

Let us go around the new museum and we come directly above the northern side of the Vatican walls. From here we can see a vast expanse of rooftops and television aerials stretching as far as Monte Mario, on the top of which is the Roman Astronomical Observatory. Much lower down is the road that leads to the entrance to the Vatican Museums. There is, however, another special entrance from above, that is from the gardens. It is where the Vatican shuffle bus which leaves St. Peter's Square for the Museums every half hour and passes through the gardens drops its passengers. Let us go a little further on however and skirt the *Palazzetto del Belvedere*, that Innocent VIII had built in the form of a fortress crowned with battlements for his summer residence on the heights of the *Mons Sancti Aegidii* (St. Giles' Mount), which is the extreme northern point of the chain of Vatican hills. About the year 1500 the first collection of antique statues was formed here in the inner courtyard of the Palazzetto and this was to become the nucleus of the great complex of the Pontifical Museums and Galleries that gradually developed.

Important guests also lodged in the Palazzetto. The most famous was Leonardo da Vinci who stayed there from 1512 until 1516. Exactly under its windows is the last

The Fountain of the Galleon serves to spout "fresh water" to extinguish the "fires of war" as the plaque attached to the wall explains, a couplet composed by Cardinal Maffeo Barberini, the future Pope Urban VIII (1623-1644). The Galleon is a picturesque allusion to the Pontiffs' mission of peace.

and most remote of the fountains, the *Fontana della Galera*, also called "*della Galea*" (Fountain of the Galleon). A galleon floats in the centre of an oval basin, a real three-master with its sailors and its cannons. In fact in the XVIth and XVIIth centuries the Popes possessed galleons of this type to protect the coasts of the Pontifical States. Still today the Vatican, as a sovereign State, has the right to send ships to sea under its own flag. Photographing the fountain with a little bit of expertise one can get the impression of a ship of normal size, whereas it is only a lead miniature with a great many little cannons that fire jets of water in every direction. This is referred to in the epigraph on the wall behind the fountain, a couplet composed by Cardinal Maffeo Barberini, the future Pope Urban VIII (1623-1644):

> *Bellica pontificium*
> *non fundit machina flammas,*
> *sed dulcem belli*
> *qua perit ignis aquam.*

> The pontifical men-of-war
> do not spout flames,
> but rather fresh water
> to quench the fires of war.

A clear allusion to the papacy's mission of peace.

Behind the fountain there is a grotto with the figure of an ancient sea-god seated among trumpet lilies, papyrus and other aquatic plants. An inscription above recalls that in 1799 Pius VI restored and embellished this fountain which was built under Paul V. The designer of the galleon was probably the Flemish architect, Jan Vasanzio, whose fountains of the Eagle and of the Sacrament we have already seen. However it was restored several times, as can be seen from Pius VI's coat-of-arms on the prow and Pius XI's on the pennant flying from the main mast.

A magnificent specimen of a giant magnolia can be seen on the right attached to the famous *Lumaca* (Snail), the spiral ramp constructed by Bramante to reach the upper floors of the Palazzetto del Belvedere without having to climb the stairs.

The Fountain of the Galleon.
The stern with a sailor sounding a trumpet.

In front of the fountain there is a panoramic terrace from which we can see the commercial area of the Vatican City below. In the foreground there are the workshops for the maintenance of official Vatican cars and alongside them a long building that houses the pharmacy and the infirmary, then comes the central telephone exchange and the central post office; in front of them, the large supermarket and the printing-works, the *Tipografia Vaticana* (the Vatican Press). The road running parallel is the *Via dei Pellegrini* (Pilgrims' Street), so named because in past centuries it was the way of access to St. Peter's for pilgrims arriving from the Monte Mario direction and also because in the street there is still the small, ancient

St. Peter's Colonnade which opens its arms
almost as if to invite us to come and stay in this little world of art, beauty,
nature, history and faith.

church of St. Pellegrino. Also on this street there are the editorial offices of the Vatican daily newspaper, *L'Osservatore Romano*, in its different language editions, as well as the canteen for employees and some workshops. There is even a small electricity substation. At the lowest point, between the parish church of St. Anne, in baroque style, and the barracks of the Swiss Guard, we can see the *Porta di S. Anna* (St. Anne's Gate), the entrance to the commercial area and at the same time the exit to the city of Rome. However, without the aforementioned "tes- sera" one cannot get into the commercial district. All we can do now is retrace our steps and go back through the English, French and Italian gardens, pass once more in front of the Governatorato and the Railway Station, cross the squares of St. Martha and of the Protomartyrs to reach our point of departure in St. Peter's Square.

Here we are embraced by the colonnade which seems to want to hold us in this singular world of peace, faith and beauty, in which each one of us has, in a manner of speaking, a spiritual right to citizenship.

Catalogue of the Principal Plants in Vatican City published by the Superintendence of the Vatican Gardens

Area	Name	Place of origin
S. MARTA	Evergreen magnolia	North America
	Eǔonymus japonicus (Spindle-tree)	Japan
	Convallaria japonica (Lily of the Valley)	Japan
	Holm oak	Mediterranean
	Italian stone pine	Indigenous
	Cypress sempervirens	Mediterranean
MOSAICO	Bux sempervirens	Indigenous
	Chinese jasmine	Japan
	Maidenhair tree	Japan
CONCHIGLIA	Common yew	North Africa
	Oleander	Mediterranean
	Austrian pine	Austria
OSSERVATORIO	American maple	North America
	Norfolk Island pine	Norfolk Islands
	Weeping willow	The Levant
	Blue gum / Eucalyptus	Tasmania
PIO XII - ULIVI	Pittosporum	China
	Dwarf palm	Indigenous
	Cedar of Lebanon	Asia Minor
	Common beech	Indigenous
	Fig	China-Japan
	Feijoa sellowiana	Brazil
	American plane	North America
	Crape myrtle	China
	Silk bark oak	Australia
	Olive	Southern Europe
RADIO VATICANA	Coral tree	Brazil
	Melaleuca	Australia
	Sago palm	Japan
	New Zealand flax	New Zealand
STEMMA	Japanese pagoda tree	Japan
	Dassylirion serratifolium	Mexico

Chronology of the Pontiffs' modifications in the Vatican Gardens

Leo IV
(847-855)
He had the Leonine Walls built around the Vatican hill to protect St. Peter's Basilica. The Leonine City, later to be called the Vatican City, developed within these walls.

Innocent III
(1198-1216)
On the hill to the north of the basilica he had the *mons saccorum* built — a fortified building complex of which one can still see the tower of the so-called House of the Gardener.

Nicholas III
(1277-1288)
He was the first Pope to make the Vatican his fixed abode. He planted a *viridarium* (kitchengarden), a *pomerium* (orchard) and a wood, all surrounded by new walls to the north west of the Leonine Walls.

Nicholas IV
(1288-1292)
His doctor Simone da Genova planted the garden "of the simples", that is of medicinal plants, thus starting the oldest botanical garden in Italy.

Urban V
(1362-1370)
Although he lived in Avignon he appointed a Custodian of the Vatican Gardens and had him plant a large vineyard.

Nicholas V
(1447-1455)
He restored the Leonine Walls, adding the battlements and the towers.

Innocent VIII
(1484-1492)
He had a summer residence built on St. Giles' Mount, at the northern extremity, the Palazzetto del Belvedere. The first ancient statues to be re-discovered were arranged in the inner garden like in an open-air museum. He also had a tower built—called Del Gallinaro—inside the hen-run, where there are now the greenhouses and the administration of the Vatican Gardens.

Julius II
(1503-1513)
He commissioned Bramante to build two long corridors to connect the Apostolic Palace with the Palazzetto del Belvedere, completed then by Pirro Ligorio. Three courtyards on three descending levels were created between these galleries and they were decorated with pots of citrus fruit trees, fountains and statues. This was the first example of a "terraced" garden.

Paul III
(1534-1549)
He started the construction of the new wall fortified with bastions slightly beyond the Leonine Walls and this has now become the boundary line of the new Vatican City State. On the northern side he planted a *"secret garden"*, hidden by a high wall, which was later to be called the "square garden" because of its shape and that of the flower-beds.

Pius IV
(1559-1565)
The "Casina di Pio IV" initiated by his predecessor Paul IV and built in the wood by Pio Ligorio, takes its name from him: a gem of mannerist renaissance art.

Pius V
(1566-1572)
A new garden of simples containing many exotic plants was laid out below the Casina di Pio IV. His personal physician, the famous Michele Mercati was appointed "herbalist", that is custodian of the botanical garden.

Gregory XIII
(1572-1585)
The Tower of the Winds was constructed on the western corridor on his orders and a first astronomical observatory was installed there.

Paul V
(1605-1621)
He had the ancient aqueduct of the Emperor Trajan restored and brought the Pauline Water into the Vatican thus enabling the construction of the large fountains: the Fountain of the Eagle, of the Sacrament and of the Galleon, the works of Jan van Santen and Martino Ferabosco.

For more than two hundred years the Popes resided in the Quirinal. During their absence the Vatican Gardens were always cared for but not modified. It was only after the return of the Popes to the Vatican that work was re-started in the gardens.

Pius IX (1846-1878)
He ordered a large monument to commemorate the First Vatican Council (1870); this was first of all erected in the Courtyard of the Belvedere and then, in a reduced form, in the garden close to the House of the Gardener. Around the statue of St. Peter giving his blessing are some marble fragments, angels' heads and reliefs which originally belonged to the large monument.

Leo XIII (1878-1903)
In his state as a "voluntary prisoner" and finding it impossible to leave the Vatican he had a summer residence prepared in the tower (first of all called the Leonine Tower, then the Tower of the Observatory and now the Radio Tower). He added to it a house, a Swiss-type chalet, for his suite, a botanical garden, a zoo and a new vineyard. On the occasion of the jubilee for his 50 years in the priesthood he received many gifts which were displayed in the gardens. What stands out among them are statues of French saints, a statue of St. Peter in chains, a bronze relief representing Pope Leo XIII with the German Emperor, Chancellor Bismarck and the King of Spain. At the top of the hill the French also built a large reproduction of the Lourdes Grotto.

Benedict XV (1914-1922)
Genoa, his native city, gave him a faithful reproduction of the shrine of Our Lady of the Guard, which is in the port, and he had it placed in the wood.

Pius XI (1922-1939)
After the signing of the Lateran Treaty, in 1929, the Vatican became an independent sovereign state (SCV). The southern part of the hill was then transformed into a "garden city". The Governatorato, the Railway Station, the Ethiopian College and the Radio-telephonic Transmitting Centre (set up by Guglielmo Marconi) were then built under the direction of the architect Giuseppe Momo. A new Picture Gallery was built on the northern side on the site of an old orange grove. On the southern slope an "Italian" garden was created and this consisted of a labyrinth of hedges and the Fountain of the Shell. In the same period a rock garden and a rose garden were also established. The Pope received as a gift from the Chinese a "Chinese Pavilion" and this is now in the wood. In 1936 he founded the Academy of Sciences and enlarged the Casina di Pio IV with an extension where he established the headquarters of the new Academy.

Pius XII (1939-1958)
The little wall that goes to the Tower of St. John was roofed-over for the Pope's daily walks. The Mexicans donated a marble group representing Our Lady of Guadalupe which was sited close to the tower itself.

John XXIII (1958-1963)
He had the Tower of St. John (dating back to the time of Nicholas V) re-built as a retreat. It now serves as a residence for the Pope's distinguished guests.

Paul VI (1963-1978)
The Pauline Museum, constructed parallel to the Picture Gallery and the Paul VI Hall designed by Pier Luigi Nervi for pontifical audiences take their names from him. The tennis court, at the extreme western angle of the Vatican walls was converted into a heliport.

John Paul II (1978-   )
To record the failed attempt on the Pope's life on the 13th May 1981 a statue of Our Lady of Fatima was erected close to the Lourdes Grotto. He received as a gift a large fragment of the Berlin Wall which has been placed in the socalled "Vignaccia" area where there was one a vineyard and where now instead are the workshops. The most recent construction (1994) is the *Mater Ecclesiae* Monastery of the Poor Clares, adjacent to the Leonine Walls and close to the Radio Tower.

Two maidenhair trees which are highly prized alongside the church of St. Stephen of the Abyssinians. In the background St. Peter's Basilica.

BIBLIOGRAPHY
IN CHRONOLOGICAL ORDER

Negro Silvio, *Papa Pecci nel suo giardino*, in: *Vaticano minore*, Roma 1963.

Jung-Inglessis Eva-Maria, *The Vatican Gardens*, in *The Vatican. Spirit and art of Christian Rome*, The Metropolitan Museum of Art, New York, N.Y. 1982.

Pietrangeli Carlo e Mancinelli Fabrizio, *Il Vaticano e i suoi giardini*, Antells, Firenze 1985.

Guide del Vaticano, Parte III: *Giardini Vaticani*, a cura di Carlo Pietrangeli, Roma 1989.

Martin Jacques, Card., *Pagine di storia nei Giardini Vaticani*, in *Vaticano sconosciuto*, Vaticano 1991.

Morello Giovanni e Piazzoni Ambrogio, *I Giardini Vaticani. Storia, Arte, Natura*, Roma 1991.

Varoli Piazza Scoppola Sofia, *I Giardini Vaticani. Prima ricognizione di un percorso*, s.d., manoscritto.

VATICAN CITY MAP

1. Information Office
2. Arch of the bell tower
3. Square of the first Roman Martyrs
4. Teutonic College and Cemetery
5. Holy Office
6. Audience Hall
7. Sacristy and House of Canons
8. Guesthouse St. Marta
9. Square of St. Marta
10. Palazzo San Carlo
11. Tribunal
12. St. Stephen of the Abyssinians
13. Mosaic Studio
14. Railway station
15. Palace of Governor
16. Ethiopian College
17. Leonine Walls
18. Grotto of Lourdes
19. Italian-style garden
20. Marconi Transmission center
21. Tower of St. John
22. Border of the Vatican City State
23. Heliport
24. Madonna of Guadalupe
25. Madonna of Fatima
26. Rose garden
27. Radio Tower
28. Mater Ecclesiae Monastery
29. Pope's orchard
30. Statue of St. Peter
31. House of the Gardener
32. Fountain of the Eagle
33. The Wood
34. Chinese pavillon
35. Garden House of Pius IV
36. Fountain of the Blessed Sacrament
37. The Mint
38. Arch of the Sentinel
39. Sistine Chapel
40. Apostolic Palaces
41. Museum Galleries
42. Tower of the Winds
43. Square garden
44. Painting Gallery
45. Museum of Paul VI
46. Greenhouses and tower of Innocent VIII
47. Berlin Wall and warehouses
48. Palazzetto del Belvedere
49. Fountain of the Galley
50. Commercial district
51. Gate of St. Anne